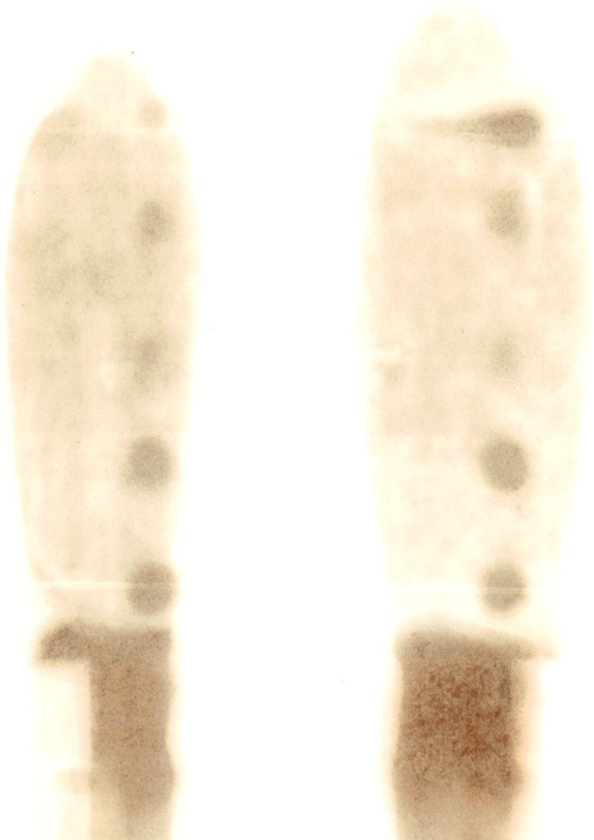

THE COVERED BRIDGE HOUSE

THE COVERED BRIDGE HOUSE

AND OTHER POEMS BY
KAYE STARBIRD

ILLUSTRATED BY
JIM ARNOSKY

FOUR WINDS PRESS NEW YORK

Library of Congress Cataloging in Publication Data

Starbird, Kaye.

The covered bridge house and other poems.
Summary: A collection of 30 poems about a variety of childhood experiences.

[1. American poetry] I. Arnosky, Jim. II. Title.
PZ8.3.S79Co 811'.5'4 79-11418
ISBN 0-590-07544-6

Published by Four Winds Press
A division of Scholastic Magazines, Inc., New York, N.Y.

Printed in the United States of America
Library of Congress Catalog Card Number: 79-11418
1 2 3 4 5 83 82 81 80 79

For
Anthony
Harley
Sean
Devon
and Casey

In the order of their arrival

Contents

THE COVERED BRIDGE HOUSE

Today

Today, though spring was overdue,
The winter world still looked the same.
Yet something in the world was new,
Something I couldn't name.

I gazed around me everywhere
And saw no changes, large or small.
There was a softness to the air,
But really that was all.

The sky above still wasn't blue.
The treetops still weren't green below,
And not a crocus struggled through
Its roof of crusted snow.

But — searching through my mind
with care —
I found myself remembering
That when a softness fills the air
Winter turns into spring.

The City and Evan

When Evan went to town from the farm
To visit his cousin, Nate,
He had a list as long as your arm
Of things to investigate.
But zoos were smelly. Museums bored him.
The traffic startled him, coming toward him.
Whenever he shopped, the clerks
ignored him,
Snubbing him left and right.
Thinking each bearded man was a bandit,
Hating the town and whoever planned it,
"How," asked Evan, "can anyone stand it,
Let alone sleep at night?"

Though nothing kept Nate awake but Evan
Thrashing around till after eleven,
Evan kept hearing the trash cans banging,
The car horns honking, the fire
trucks clanging,
Whistles and bells and sirens and such,
All of which bothered Evan so much
That — finding the city minus charm —
Evan returned to the farm.

The Country and Nate

This Easter, Nate left town for a change
And traveled to Evan's farm,
But everything there was either strange
Or filled him full of alarm.
The pigs were smelly. The chickens
bored him.
The horses startled him, coming toward him,
And — when he fished — the fishes
ignored him,
Not acting much impressed.
The sun shone down, but it shone
too brightly.
The barns were big, but the stalls unsightly,
And — even worse — were the awful nightly
Noises that wrecked his rest.

He'd lie in bed while Evan was dreaming
And hear the night birds screeching
and screaming,
The peepers peeping, the river splashing,
And umpteen tree limbs bumping and
crashing.
So after a week of all that racket,
He got his bag and began to pack it;
And — gazing back at the farm with pity —
Nate returned to the city.

The Ride

Susie Skinner rode her horse
From Stowe to Troy and back,
And — though she rode for miles
    and miles —
Susie didn't keep track.
And now when Susie's friends come by
And ask her with a squeal:
How did she *like* her Famous Ride?
Susie says, "No big deal."

Susie, the morning Susie left,
Didn't do much deciding,
She just looked out and thought the day
A perfect day for riding.
And ten hours later, Susie phoned
Her mother, Mrs. Skinner,
Saying she might be gone awhile
And not to save her dinner.

That was the evening Susie got
Five lovely apples, free,
And gave a couple to her horse
And ate the other three.
And, after sleeping on a hill,
Susie remarked at dawn:
"Another perfect riding day!"
And started riding on.

And since she sang and waved a lot
And never acted choosy,
Many a stranger cooked a meal
Or loaned a bed to Susie.
Otherwise, Susie found a field
Away from towns and cars
And lay there in her sleeping bag
Munching on candy bars.

It's hard to say when Susie took
A sudden highway fork
And noticed she was riding through
The town of Troy, New York.
Susie just says she telephoned
To Stowe, Vermont . . . and then
She simply turned her horse around
And rode back home again.

Jump Rope Song

Heather has four ruby rings.
Heather has three pearly lockets.
Heather has — plus other things —
Two fur coats with velvet pockets.
Heather has a Paris purse
Full of cash she never spends.
I should mention something worse.
Heather has no friends.

Kids don't mind her ruby rings.
Kids don't mind her pearly lockets.
Kids don't mind the other things
Like her coats with velvet pockets.
Kids don't mind her Paris purse
Full of cash and made of leather.
What kids mind is something worse.
What they mind is Heather.

For, in spite of gems and furs
(Plus a purse in good condition),
Heather — with that will of hers —
Has a horrid disposition.
Heather, much to Heather's loss,
Always wants to run the show;
And if Heather isn't boss,
Heather sulks. And so . . .

Though she has four ruby rings,
Though she has three pearly lockets,
Though she has — plus other things —
Two fur coats with velvet pockets,
Also cash she never spends
In a Paris purse of leather,
When it comes to having friends,
Heather just has Heather.

Mother

My mother says
If the neighbor boys
Keep having quarrels
And making noise,
She'll surely jump right out of her skin.
But I say, "Don't,"
And I hope she won't
Unless she's able to jump back in.

The World's Best Hopper

The winter when Grace began to ski
And slipped on the slopes and smashed her knee,
She had some crutches to lift her cast,
But Grace got rid of the crutches fast.
We all imagined her falling flat
With nothing handy to keep her propped,
But Grace did something smarter than that.
Wherever she wished to go
She hopped.

For sixteen weeks
Till her kneecap mended
Her skill at hopping
Was really splendid.
She hopped up stairways
And over walls.
In gym, she hopped
After volleyballs;
So I believe the title was proper
When people named her
'The World's Best Hopper.'

The time I remember most is once
When Grace was still in her leg-cast months
And challenged me to a hopping race.
"We'll only go round the block," said Grace.
Then, "Ready, set, GO!" was what she said,
And off she started
Full speed ahead.

I started, too, but I took one hop
And caught my shoe in a manhole top
And down I went
On the hard cement
In front of Flora's Finery Shop.
And there I stayed till the winner, Grace,
Came hopping back to our starting place
And said to me, as I sat and hurt,
"What are you *doing* in all that dirt?"

"The thing I'm doing," I said, "is dropping
Whatever plans I had about hopping.
For you, it may be a useful pastime;
But — me — I've hopped for the first and
    last time,
So what I'll be is a hopping-stopper,
While you keep being
'The World's Best Hopper.' "

The Blizzard

I can't forget the second night of the snow,
For that's the night when the blizzard
cut the power,
The night the electric clocks said: five-of-six,
And none of them in the city struck the hour,
Not even the plain one over City Hall,
Not even the fancy one in St. Paul's tower.

A night like that can shake your
sureness in things,
For though my mother handed us
each a sweater
And lighted some candles, while my
brother sat
Stroking and stroking our nervous Irish setter,
And Father cooked a steak on the
parlor hearth
Somehow, I kept feeling worse instead
of better.
For time stood still (which time isn't
meant to do)
And seemed a problem no one could ever fix.
And, even after the lights went on again
And so did the furnace, time kept
playing tricks.
For instance, it was twelve by my silver watch
When all the electric clocks in town struck six.

The Wind

In spring, the wind's a sneaky wind,
A tricky wind,
A freaky wind,
A wind that hides around the bends
And doesn't die, but just pretends;
So if you stroll into a street
Out of a quiet lane,
All of a sudden you can meet
A smallish hurricane.

And as the grown-ups gasp and cough
Or grumble when their hats blow off,
And housewives clutch their grocery sacks
While all their hairdos come unpinned . . .
We kids — each time the wind attacks —
Just stretch our arms and turn our backs.
And then we giggle and relax
And lean against the wind.

Watch Out!

Since Beverly likes to frighten kids
And Beverly's mind is sly,
I really hated rooming with her
This summer at Camp Blue Sky.
I mean, because I was new at camp
And seemed like an easy mark,
One time she caught a minnow and yelled:
"Watch *out*! It's a baby shark!"

Another thing that Beverly did
In order to have her fun
Was jab her thumb in my back at night
And yell: "Watch out! It's a gun!"
For, though I was fairly sure that guns
(Like lollypops hidden cleverly)
Were banned in the True Blue honor rules,
The rules never bothered Beverly.

The counselors tried to tame her down
And Beverly changed her talk
By saying about a hen she caught:
"Please notice my stunted hawk."
However, her tameness disappeared
The noon of our final day
When we were having our Banquet lunch
Before the water ballet.

That's when Beverly lay in the loft
Above the room where we sat
And hung a mouse through a hole and yelled:
"Watch *out*! It's a wingless bat!"
And while she swung it above our soup
By holding its tail with pliers,
She pretty much wrecked the appetites
Of all of us Camp-Blue-Sky-ers.

So, though I was fond of Camp Blue Sky
And liked the program a lot,
In case I'm going again next year
I hope that Beverly's not.

The Ant in the Windmill

Over in the valley
In an age gone by
Someone built a windmill
That is high, high, high.
Hidden in the windmill
Are some steps to climb,
Only, though, for climbers
With the strength and time.

One day when I struggled
Up the last steep stair,
Suddenly I noticed
That an ant was there.
Seeing it reclining
On a rafter tip,
I began to wonder
How it made the trip.

Crawling up the staircase?
Crawling up the wall?
Either way it traveled
Was a long, hard crawl.
Therefore, I decided
As I paused to pant:
Nothing is a problem
To a strong-willed ant.

So it simply figured
It would move and did,
And — without a notion
It would slip and skid —
Finally the insect
With its ant-eyes glowing
Found itself arriving
Where it planned on going.

Ruth

When Ruth
Broke a tooth
And couldn't bite,
She raced to her dentist, Dr. Dwight,
Who looked concerned while she
murmured, "Ouch,"
And raised her up on his dental couch
And said, as he gave her mouth a hunt,
"We seem to have trouble here in front."

And Ruth, a girl who's pretty outspoken,
Said, "Sure, there's trouble. My tooth
is broken.
But kindly stick to the facts," said she.
"Since *I* have the trouble, don't say 'we.' "

The dentist poked at her tooth and drilled it,
And said to Ruth, who frowned as he filled it,
"I'm happy our tooth turned out all right."

And Ruth said patiently, "Dr. Dwight,
I'm mighty grateful. The tooth feels fine,
Except it isn't *our* tooth. It's mine."

For Ruth believes
In telling the truth
Even about a broken tooth.

The Spelling Test

One morning in a spelling test
The teacher said to Hugh:
"I have a word for you to spell.
The word is 'kangaroo.' "
But Hugh was puzzled by the word
Which wasn't one he knew,
So, when he wrote it on the board,
He printed "kannagrue."

"No, NO! Go take your seat again,"
The teacher said to Hugh,
"And take along this copy card.
The card says 'kangaroo.'
Then get your pencil out," she said,
"And get your notebook, too.
And write the word a hundred times
And tell me when you're through."

So Hugh did just exactly what
The teacher told him to,
And, when he handed in his work,
The teacher said to Hugh:
"I hope you know your spelling now."
And Hugh said, "Yes, I do,"
Then — walking bravely to the board —
He printed "kannagrue."

I Dreamed I Visited Buzzard's Bay

I dreamed I visited Buzzard's Bay
Where waves were whooshing and hurtling
And heard a sad lady turtle say:
"I'm pretty fed up with turtling.
Although I work on a home each year
And hide my eggs in the dunes,
They all get eaten by buzzards here
Or else by the smart raccoons.

"My mate," she added, giving a sob,
"Went off when I kept complaining,
So I suppose I should get a job,
Except that I have no training.
When I was a young and foolish girl
I wanted to be a dancer;
But — since I never could leap or whirl —
That plainly wasn't the answer."

The turtle gave me a look of pain,
But after a while she brightened
And said, "I'm just not using my brain
Because I'm too sad and frightened.
So toodle-dee-oo and what the heck,
I'm sick of being a loser.
With both a roof and a lower deck,
I *could* be a cabin cruiser!"

Then, looking relieved as well as brave,
"That's *just* what I'll be," she cried,
And — as she hopped an outgoing wave —
She giggled, "Gosh, what a ride!"
And later she shouted from afar,
"I'm calling you ship-to-shore.
I think I'm headed for Zanzibar,
So toodle-dee-oo once more."

And, starting off on her first big cruise,
The turtle vanished away,
Because she didn't honestly choose
To hang around Buzzard's Bay.
And, though she left as a last resort,
I'm sure she enjoys her trips
And now is sailing from port to port
As proudly as other ships.

The Pole Bean Tent

I heard about a pole bean tent
From Uncle Walt the time he came.
So back in May I planted beans
Around a sturdy pup-tent frame
And strung some strings from side to side
Out from the roof bar like an 'A,'
And — when the bean stems climbed
the strings —
My little tent turned out okay.

And now I rest, when days are hot,
There where the world is cool and green,
The peakéd roof, the grass below
And both the slanty walls between;
And, if I'm feeling emptyish,
I reach and pick myself a bean.

Yet, even though I tried to mind
The building rules of Uncle Walt's
And really built a super tent,
I must admit it has its faults.
So, if you're planning such a place,
Expect some losses with your gains,
And realize a tent of leaves
Is mighty leaky when it rains.

The Twins

Though Timmy is a pleasant boy
And Howard loves a riot,
The Kent twins look so much alike
That — when the two are quiet —
Sometimes the only way to tell
The good twin from the mean one
Is: Timmy wears an orange belt
And Howard wears a green one.

At lunch, it's easy to decide
Which of the twins is Timmy,
When Timmy says: "Please pass the salt,"
And Howard hollers, "Gimmee!"
However, in the locker room,
After the twins have showered,
Until they buckle on their belts
I think that Timmy's Howard.

At least, I *did* before the day
I got my share of welts
Because I didn't realize
The twins had switched their belts.
And when I joked with Timmy Kent
And slapped his back, he glowered
And socked me in the jaw, which proved
Timmy was really Howard.

What happened next to Howard Kent
Was justice, I suppose,
For when I socked him back again
He got a broken nose;
And even though his nose has healed
The middle part is bent,
So lately I can always tell
Timmy from Howard Kent.

Wendy in Winter

No wonder Wendy's coat blew off.
She didn't have it zipped.
And — since she didn't watch for slush —
No wonder Wendy slipped.
No wonder Wendy froze her feet
Although her boots were lined,
Because when Wendy left for school
She left her boots behind.
And since she didn't dodge the ice
That sagged an apple bough,
No wonder Wendy's hatless head
Has seven stitches now.

Artie

Since Artie Dole
Can't seem to control
His busy imagination,
Last year our teacher, Miss Cass, was sure
He'd ruin our education.

It all began the morning Miss Cass
(Who always liked new worlds to explore)
Spread open a map and asked the class:
Could anyone point to Singapore?
And Artie arose
And said, "Gee whiz.
*Any*one knows
Where Singapore is.
In case you ever want to arrive
You borrow an open truck to drive,
And after you've bounced through
rocks and crags
Until your trouser bottoms are rags,
You head northwest at a motor lodge
And — if a lion attacks — you dodge
And leave the truck when the engine quits
And find a jungle helmet that fits
And cross a desert and then some hills
Where birds keep biting you with their bills;
And while you're living on gopher eggs
And snakes keep winding around your legs,
Although you're sick with the chickenpox
You board a raft near some seaside docks
And pole the raft till some friendly apes
Come swooping down in their batman capes
And flap their capes and steer you to shore.
And that's how you get to Singapore."

As Artie stopped with a modest smile,
Our teacher looked at him goggle-eyed
And wouldn't let him talk for a while
Even though Artie often tried.

In fact, it wasn't until November,
The day we described our Halloweens,
That Artie's speech was one to remember
And not the nicest, by any means.
Though most of us felt a sort of dread
When Artie Dole got into the act.
"I went to a party," Artie said,
"A witches' party, to be exact.
We even had it outdoors," said Artie,
"In kind of a drippy, creepy cave,
Because it wasn't a *people* party.
It was a party some witches *gave*.
We all made stew, and believe-you-me
It was a horrible recipe.

"We started," he said," with crankcase oil,
And while three witches sang, 'Boil, stew, boil,'
We put ten tadpoles into the pot
And seventeen rats the Head Witch shot
And fourteen rotten banana peels
And maybe a dozen slimy eels
And twenty cobras we had to crush
And half a bucket of mule-meat mush
And plenty of slugs and caterpillars
And worms and ants in the way of fillers
And donkey tails
And the spouts of whales
And lots of leftover fingernails
And eagle claws
And crocodile jaws
And THEN," said Artie, after a pause,
"We added some toads from dirty ditches
And ALL *of the Uninvited Witches*!"

As Artie finished his speech with style
And sat again with his same old smile,
Although a lot of us just said, "Ick,"
Isabel Jones got terribly sick;
And poor Miss Cass, with her wits half gone,
Announced to Artie, *"From this day on*
Whatever you're thinking, don't recite it.
Take out your pencil and pad, and write it!"
And Artie did what the teacher said,
And everyone's life got somewhat brighter
When Artie Dole
Got under control
And ended up as the school's best writer.

The Covered Bridge House

Because there's a race
For living space,
I have a wonderful scheme.
I'm planning to own a covered bridge
Up over a running stream.
Except for some doors on entry halls,
I'll board up the ends with planks
And put some windows upon the walls
That face away from the banks.

No buildings are apt to crowd me there
With nothing to build them on;
And, since my yard will be waves and air,
I won't need to mow the lawn.
I'll have a skylight where raindrops skid
And clouds look in as they sail
And cut a floor hole (one with a lid)
For filling my water pail.

And though, in winter, I'll skate a lot
Or read from morning till twilight
Before I climb on my cozy cot
To watch the moon through my skylight . . .
In spring, I'll open my floor hole wide
And fish through it for my supper
And later scrape the scraps in the tide,
Or — if I'm a cleaner-upper —

I'll hang my pans in a net on string
And maybe my laundry, too;
And when it's summer, I'll swim and sing
Or paddle my red canoe.
And if the shivering mice sneak in
When summer changes to fall,
I'll say to each mouse:
"Enjoy my house.
There's room enough for us all."

Loring

When Loring Bronson, a fifth-grade kid,
Was born eleven years back,
I'll bet the very first thing he did
Was pile some books in a pyramid
And read his way through the stack.
And, since his reading room *still* is stacked
With books from ceiling to flooring,
In case you're hazy on any fact
And want it fast and want it exact,
—Ask Loring.

For instance, if you find you forget
The present size of the national debt
Or what the weather's like in Tibet
Or which way the Danube flows,
Or how many votes ex-President Johnson
Got in Idaho or Wisconsin,
Ask the answer from Loring Bronson.
—Loring knows.

Loring knows what the weight of a gnat is,
Knows what the height of a Bishop's hat is,
Knows why a tree sloth (whatever *that* is)
Happens to have three toes.
Any old knowledge that's odd or weird
Like why the jungle's never been cleared
Or why an Indian has no beard,
—Loring knows.

Faced with a question, however tough,
He gives it his concentration,
And — when he thinks he's
answered enough —
He goes on busily reading stuff
And storing up information.
And, though I've asked in a pleasant tone,
The reason he *does* the storing
His answer (which he tends to postpone)
Seems to be one that's not even known
By Loring.

The Stranger

An old man came to church one day
Dressed in a tie and coat,
And when the hymns began to play
He never sang a note.
And after church, when Preacher Lyme
Remarked: "You're not a singer?"
The stranger answered: "No, sir, I'm
A ringer.

"That is," he said, "I sing off-key
Because I'm deaf at times,
But in my youth I used to be
The ringer of the chimes.
And though today my ears have flaws
And fail me in a crowd,
I long to ring the chimes because
They're loud."

"Why don't you then?" asked Preacher Lyme,
"Or try it, anyhow.
If you could ring them in your prime,
You ought to ring them now.
Our Sunday Chimer leaves at noon.
Because he likes to fish.
So ring the chimes. Ring any tune
You wish."

The preacher's offer pleased the man,
Who climbed the belfry slowly
And — after he arrived — began
With music calm and holy.
But when the clock struck one o'clock
And tolled a single toll,
He switched to Western tunes and rock-
And-roll.

Then, never pausing for a break,
He played some jazz and marches
So fiercely that they seemed to shake
The church's aisles and arches.
With songs that saddened, songs
that cheered,
He played till dusk that Sunday,
And then he simply disappeared
On Monday.

I don't know why or where he went
After he rang "A-men"
Or if the stranger ever meant
To come this way again.
But, though he chose to disappear
To other towns or climes
And hasn't been around all year,
The tunes he played were true and clear;
And, in my mind, I still can hear
The chimes.

That Morning in June

That morning in June when I wakened
    at sunrise
And walked alone,
I followed a path through the country,
    half-hidden
And overgrown,
Where everything, everywhere glittered
    and sparkled.
Everything shone.

Along with the shimmering grass near
    the dewy
Path that I took,
The tipped-over bowl of the sky had
    a gleaming
And polished look,
And so did the glimmering fishes
    that circled
The see-through brook.

It seemed as if Someone Important
had ordered
The world to shine.
And suddenly everything listened
and glistened,
Each leaf, each vine
And even the numberless needles
on every
Steeple-topped pine.

In case (when I'm older) I find I'm forgetful
Of things I've known,
I hope I'll remember forever that morning
I walked alone,
That morning when everything,
everywhere sparkled.
Everything shone.

The Cat Lady

Miss Flynn has over thirty cats.
At first she had two kittens,
A girl and boy
For fun and joy
Named Sport and Millie Mittens.

That April, Sport
And Mitt (for short)
Had babies: Scare and Lapkins,
Both born in style
Upon a pile
Of newly laundered napkins.

Then Lap and Scare
Became a pair
(Since girl cats mate with brothers)
Producing Puff
And Flounce and Fluff
And Blink and Moon and others.

And when *that* batch
Played mix-and-match
Cats crowded every nook,
And one named Hum
Kept peering from
Miss Flynn's best pocketbook.

And since their owner loves them all
And treats her home as theirs,
We're glad Miss Flynn
Did not begin
With two baboons or bears.

Slim Slater

Slim Slater lives in a camper
That serves as a house and car,
And, in his movable household
That carries him near and far,
He keeps no extra possessions
Except for a green guitar.

Before Slim travels each morning
Through sunshine or rain or snow,
He strokes his guitar a minute,
Then strums it an hour or so,
And sings to his strumming music
A ballad called "Here we go."

And when he stops in the evening
He squints at the first white star
And — even before his supper —
He picks up his green guitar
And sings to the dusk or sunset
A ballad called "Here we are."

And, since he has no companions
To keep him from being free,
When people who hear his ballads
Ask: "Who does he mean by ' We'?"
Slim Slater quietly answers,
"My camper, guitar and me."

So Slim, with countries to cover,
Continues to ride and roam,
And whether he drives his camper
To Mexico, Maine, or Nome,
Slim Slater is never homesick
Because he is always home.

As Soon as the Stars Are Suburbs

As soon as the stars are suburbs
And Mars is merely a jaunt
And people from earth can travel
Wherever and how they want . . .

I think, in choosing a journey,
I'll polish and oil my bike
And take a ride
Through the countryside,
A trip I happen to like.

Eddie Wasn't Ready

Mary and Mike and Eleanor
And Gus and Eddie Doane
Were going with their parents
On a trip to Yellowstone.
The car was revved and running,
But the car was standing steady,
Mainly because the other Doanes
Were waiting there for Eddie.
Eddie had let the puppy loose
(Though he was meant to mind it)
So everybody fidgeted
While Eddie went to find it.

Mary and Eleanor and Gus
And Eddie Doane and Mike
Decided Sunday morning
They were going on a hike.
But when the five had packed their packs
With what was necessary,
And Mike and Eleanor were dressed
And also Gus and Mary . . .
They had to wait for You-Know-Who,
And so they sat and sat
Till Eddie found his hiking boots
And, after that, his hat.

Eleanor Doane and Eddie Doane
And Mary, Mike and Gus
Were going off to Boston
On a special touring bus.
But Eddie's money clip was lost,
And while he searched about him
And turned the household upside down,
The others left without him.
So now, as Eddie suffers
From a blow that's hard to soften,
He *may* have learned that Eddie
Wasn't ready
once
too
often.

The Corner Newsman

It's strange about the newsman,
The one named Joe Malloy.
Along with having little
To laugh at or enjoy,
Why doesn't he wear mittens?
Why is he known as "Boy"?

He must be over sixty,
Yet all day long he stands
Selling whatever papers
The passing crowd demands
And blowing in the winter
Upon his chilly hands.

Sometimes I hate the people
On foot or in a car
Who holler, "Boy, *The Herald*!"
Or "Boy, I want *The Star*,"
While I keep thinking, thinking
How cold his fingers are.

That's why with Christmas coming
And all the trees aglow,
I bought some furry mittens
And tied them with a bow
And went around this evening
And offered them to Joe.

"Why, thank you, little lady,"
He said and stroked the fur;
And, though I wasn't certain
Just what his feelings were,
I said to him, "You're welcome.
A merry Christmas, sir."

Miss Casper's Cow

Because Miss Casper gets annoyed
As progress moves ahead,
When gas got scarce she sold her cars
And bought a bike, instead.
And since she hates all store-bought milk
And never uses any,
Today she keeps in her garage
A Jersey cow named Jenny
And pays her former driver now
To tend and milk her private cow.

When Jenny came and saw the grass
Between the house and road,
She chewed Miss Casper's fenced-in lawn
Till it was neatly mowed.
And though her stomach slowly grew
As round as a balloon,
It simply meant that Jenny planned
To be a mother soon.

And, afterward, when Jenny had
A big-eyed female calf,
Miss Casper, who was looking on,
Began to smile and laugh
And said (while giving Jenny's neck
A friendly neck massage),
"How nice to have a second cow
In my two-cow garage."

Little Lenore

Little Lenore
Who is barely four
And can't stand people who preach
Is planning to have a Coke machine
Installed within easy reach.

And ever since she went to the Fair
With all of its sights and rides,
Little Lenore is planning to have
A number of things, besides.

She's thinking of planting cotton fields
That only grow cotton candy
And figures a private Ferris wheel
Would frequently come in handy.

She already has a special friend,
A make-believe helper, Neal,
Who's willing to tend her cotton fields
And manage her Ferris wheel.

He'll also fill up her Coke machine
And everything else like that.
And then, if people are mean to her
Like making her feed the cat . . .

She'll take a seat in her Ferris wheel,
And Neal will get it to rise
And stop her chair
High up in the air
Till people apologize.

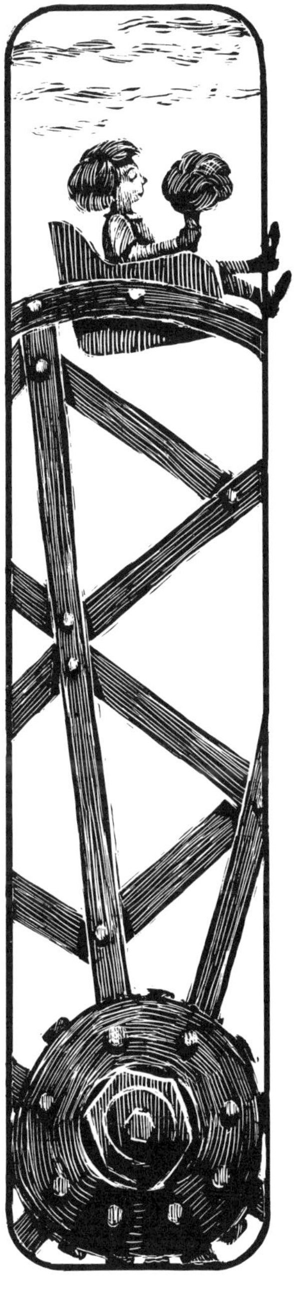

Sparrows

A hummingbird hums.
A woodpecker drums.
A gull is graceful in flight.
A jay finds fighting
Pretty exciting
And licks every bird in sight.
A swallow swoops
In up-and-down loops
And seldom lights on the ground.
But take a sparrow
Whose world is narrow.
A sparrow just hangs around.

A partridge whirs
Through the pines and firs.
A chicadee's ways are cute.
A pigeon coos
And an owl hoo-hoos
Whenever it gives a hoot.
A crow steals corn
From the year it's born,
Then hides where it can't be found.
A sparrow, though,
Doesn't come or go.
A sparrow just hangs around.

You Can't Get Rags from Ragweed

If you're a true believer,
I'll warn you in advance:
You can't get rags from Ragweed
Or milk from Milkweed plants.

You can't use Lady's Slippers
For shoes or dancing pumps,
And — as for Johnny-jump-ups —
There isn't one that jumps.

Such names of weeds and blossoms
Are harmless, I expect,
But since they're only pretty
And not a bit correct . . .

Don't ever set your wristwatch
When Four-o'Clocks say four
Or think that Tiger Lilies
Will rush at you and roar.

And never wait for Bluebells
To ring outside your gate,
For — if you do — you're likely
To have a long, long wait.

The Gardener

When Grandpa couldn't hoe or spade
Because his legs kept swelling,
He had a little greenhouse made
And hitched it to his dwelling.
And now he spends his waking hours
There in his new glass room,
Tending and talking to the flowers
And urging them to bloom.

And since my grandpa knows the needs
Of all the plants he grows from seeds . . .

He treats each blossom like a pet
And — limping as he goes —
He says: "Good morning, Violet,"
Or "Have some water, Rose."
There's always praise in Grandpa's voice
When leaves and buds unfold,
But, if my grandpa has no choice,
He's pretty apt to scold.

For instance, once he said to Fern
(Who takes her time at minding),
"Stop staying wound inside your urn!"
And Fern began unwinding.
And once when Daisy stooped too low
He told her, "Don't be lazy!
Straighten your droopy stem and show
You're proud to be a daisy!"

And Daisy must have heard his talk
Because she straightened up her stalk.

So even if my grandpa's ways
Make certain people frown,
They all admit he seems to raise
The finest plants in town.
And, when I help him with his chores,
He says to me: "My dear,
Although the seasons change outdoors,
It's always springtime here."

The Sleepers

When Jimbo Jeep and his mutt, Muldoon,
Decided one day to sleep till noon,
Said Jimbo Jeep to his private pup,
"I see no reason for getting up,
So let's just stay in this cozy bed.
You at the foot and me at the head."

Noon turned to night, and the two slept on,
And — after a week had come and gone —
"I honestly think," said Jimbo Jeep,
"We both could do with a bit more sleep."
Then he and his dog began to snore
And slept for another month or more.

And that's how it went from March till June
With Jimbo Jeep and his mutt, Muldoon.
Their only caller was Grocer Ted
Who made deliveries next to the bed
And brought them bargains — as
grocers do —
Like yesterday's bread and tasteless stew.

I guess it was early in July
When Grocer Ted refused to come by.
"You owe me cash, and your bill is steep,"
Said Ted the Grocer to Jimbo Jeep.
"You'd better get dressed and pay your bill."
And Jimbo said, "If I must, I will."

So Jimbo Jeep announced to his pup,
"I figure it's time we both got up."
And — after giving the quilts a yank —
He took his dog and went to the bank
And carried a check to Grocer Ted.
Then he and Muldoon went back to bed.

The Riddle

Why does a chicken cross the road?
Not long ago, I replied:
A chicken crosses because it wants
To get to the other side.

But, seeing the four-lane roads today,
I think — to answer the riddle —
I'd say a chicken crosses the road
To end up dead in the middle.

I'd also say from watching the cars
That speed while the traffic thickens:
If too many chickens cross the road
The world won't have any chickens.

The Birds

I wonder how birds, going back and forth,
Decide which moment to leave the north.

The other day when the autumn sun
Still shone the way it had always done,
The season suddenly left for good
With all of its warmth and shine,
When scores of birds flew out of the wood
Onto the telephone line.

They huddled there as the light went out,
Their feathers fluffed by the breeze,
As if they wanted to think about
Their city of empty trees,
The city where some had raised their young
And all had nested and lived and sung.

And then, although not one of them stirred
To make a signal or chirp a word,
They rose in a flock and swooped and veered
And headed southward and disappeared.

But how did they know? How did
they know
Exactly when it was time to go?

There wasn't a cloud to give them warning,
No sight that I saw, no sign,
Yet there was snow on the ground
next morning
Under the telephone line.